Traditional Irish Music
for the
Bagpipe

Dave Rickard

Ossian Publications

FOREWORD

About fifteen years ago I became interested in collecting and 'setting' Irish Traditional Music for the bagpipes. Over the years of playing these tunes I received so many requests for copies, that I found I could not comply with them and I therefore had the idea of compiling this collection.

I have included reels, jigs, polkas, slides and airs, all with metronome indications, because it is important to play Irish dance tunes at the right tempo, as a lot of the 'feel' can be lost by playing too fast or too slow. In two of the tunes I have included the controversial 'flat' C. I have marked its occurrence in each case with an asterisk and have explained, for those who don't already know, how it is played.

Finally, I would like to thank my good friend Seán Donnelly for all his help in compiling this collection and also to mention the late Breandán Breathnach, who greatly encouraged me in my endeavours.

Dave Rickard

Published by
Ossian Publications

Exclusive Distributors:
Hal Leonard,
7777 West Bluemound Road,
Milwaukee, WI 53213
Email: info@halleonard.com
Hal Leonard Europe Limited,
42 Wigmore Street Maryleborne,
London, WIU 2 RY
Email: info@halleonardeurope.com
Hal Leonard Australia Pty. Ltd.
4 Lentara Court Cheltenham,
Victoria, 9132 Australia
Email: info@halleonard.com.au

Order No. OMB45
ISBN 0-946005-74-5

Printed in EU.

www.halleonard.com

The Clare Jig

♩. = 127 Double Jig

Bill Harte's Jig

♩. = 127 Double Jig

Rakish Paddy

♩ = 200 min. Reel

The Humours of Tulla

♩ = 200 min. Reel

The First Slip

♩. = 144 Slip Jig

The Humours of Whiskey (1)

♩. = 144 Slip Jig

8

The Cook in the Kitchen

♩. = 127   Double Jig

❋ This C note is played with the B finger down on the chanter and the little finger raised.

Tear the Calico

♩ = 200 min.   Reel

Kevin's Polka

This C note is played with the B finger down on the chanter and the little finger raised.

Sweeney's

♩ = 137 Polka

The Langstern Pony

♩. = 127   Double Jig

♩ = 200 min   Reel

The Glass of Beer

13

Merrily Kiss the Quaker's Wife

♩.= 127 Double Jig

The Hare in the Corn

The Humours of Whiskey (2)

Fraher's Jig

♩. = 120 Jig

Cis Ní Liatháin

♩. = 137 Single Jig

The Silver Spear

♩ = 200 min.   Reel

Johnny Mickey Barry's

Is maith le Nora

Where is the Cat

♩. = 137 Slide

Pay the Reckoning

♩. = 127 Double Jig

19

The Swallow's Tail

♩ = 200 min.   Reel

Johnnie Cope

♩ = 84 Hornpipe

The Flags of Dublin

♩ = 200 min. Reel

Lord Ramsey's

♩ = 200 min. Reel

22

The Three Little Drummers

♩.= 127   Double Jig

The Blarney Pilgrim

♩. = 127   Double Jig

O'Dalaigh's

♩ = 137 Polka

All the way to Galway

♩ = 200 min. Reel

♩. = 127 Double Jig

The Lark in the Morning

27

The Back of the Haggard

♩ = 137 Polka

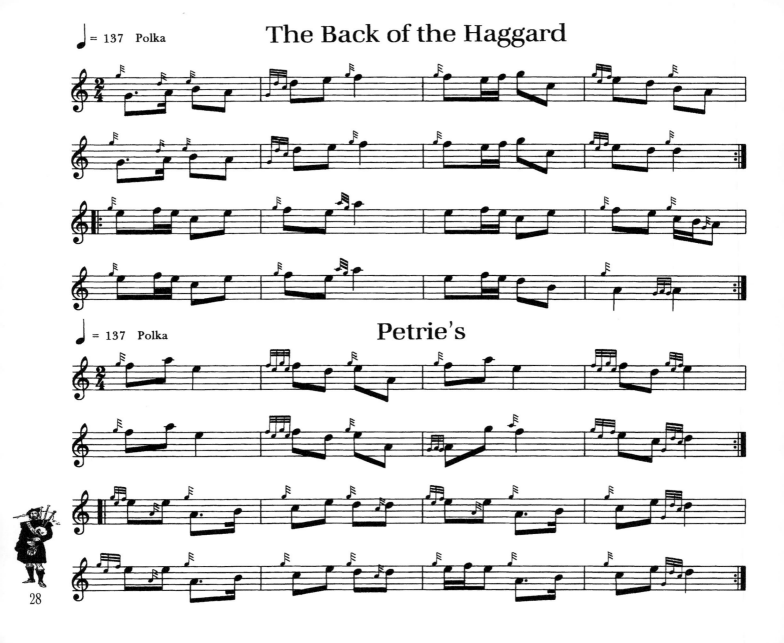

Petrie's

♩ = 137 Polka

28

Keeffe's Slide

♪. = 137 Slide

O the Britches full of Stitches

♩ = 137 Polka

29

An Bhrosna

Maggie Shanley's

30

O'Sullivan's March

Art O'Keefe's

♩. = 137   Slide

Mo Ghile Mear

♩ = 104   Air

An Mhaighdean Mhara

♩ = 60 Air

Eibhli Geal Ciuin Ni Cearbhaill

♩. = 42 Air

33

O'Dubhshlaine's Jig

♩. = 127

The Eagle's Whistle

March

34

Mairseáil Rí Laoise

The Boys of Malin

♩ = 200 min.   Reel

Tiocfaidh tú Abhaile liom

♩.= 127 Double Jig

The Gravel Walk

♩ = 200 Reel

37

Samhradh Samhradh

Aoibhneas Éilís Ní Cheallaigh